Mythologies

Monsters

John Malam

QED

QED Publishing

Copyright © QED Publishing 2009

First published in the UK in 2009 by
QED Publishing
A Quarto Group company
226 City Road
London EC1V 2TT

A catalogue record for this book is available from
the British Library.

ISBN 978 1 84835 184 4

Author John Malam
Editor Amanda Learmonth
Designer Lisa Peacock
Illustrator Vincent Follenn

Publisher Steve Evans
Creative Director Zeta Davies
Managing Editor Amanda Askew

Printed and bound in China

Picture credits
(t=top, b=bottom, l=left, r=right, c=centre, fc=front cover)
Alamy Images 5cr The Natural History Museum, 12 North
Wind Picture Archives
Bridgeman Art Library 5br Ashmolean Museum, University of
Oxford, UK, 18 British Library, London, UK/British Library
Board
Corbis 29 Ainaco
Getty Images 19br The Bridgeman Art Library/Boleslas Biegas
Mary Evans Picture Library 13t
Photolibrary 15 Thomas Hallstein, 26 Walter Bibikow, 27
Loraine Wilson
Scala Archive 21t, 23
Shutterstock 4b Janprchal, 11b Arlen E Breiholz, 17t
Canismaior
Temple University/ College of Liberal Arts 7t
Topham Picturepoint 2, 4t Charles Walker, 5tl Charles Walker,
5bc Fortean, 9b Alinari, 13b Charles Walker, 17b Charles
Walker, 25
Werner Foreman 5cc Christie's, London

Words in **bold** are explained
in the glossary on page 30.

CONTENTS

The world of monsters

The world's myths are full of creatures that are very different from those in real life. As they look strange and scary to us, we call them monsters.

Monsters come from a storyteller's imagination. Every time a story is told, the monster in the storyteller's mind grows bigger and scarier. It reaches a point when it's as big and as bad as it needs to be, and that's how it stays.

Myths about monsters have been told for thousands of years, by people all over the world. Many of these myths, such as those of the ancient Greeks from 2500 years ago, have become well known.

⬆ The **werewolf** is a human that changes into a wolf during a full moon.

Clay creatures

In the Middle Ages in Europe (about 800 years ago), Jewish folklore told of a human-like monster called a **golem** (meaning 'a clod of earth'). It was a servant that helped and protected its human master.

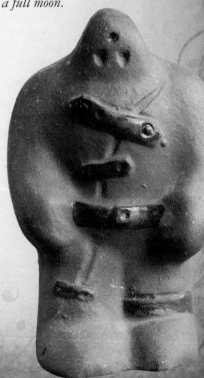

➡ A golem was formed from clay, and came to life when it was put under a spell.

Who's who among monsters?

Flying Head
This is a giant head with wings for ears, wild hair, fiery eyes and rows of pointed fangs.

Griffin
A beast with the body of a lion and the head and wings of an eagle.

Great Serpent
A massive snake with a red head and scales of many colours.

Minotaur
This monster has the body of a man and the head of a bull.

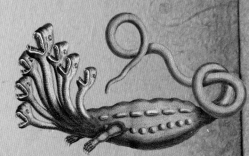

Hydra
A giant serpent with many heads and poisonous blood.

Kraken
This enormous, horned sea monster dragged ships down to the seabed.

Harpy
A flying creature with the legs and wings of a vulture and the head and body of a woman.

Cerberus
A giant dog with three heads, each of which was covered in snakes.

Monsters with many heads

Some of the weirdest-looking monsters ever described are ones that have many heads.

The ancient Greeks told stories about Cerberus, a fierce, three-headed dog. They also believed in the **Chimera**, which was a cross between a goat, a lion and a serpent, with heads growing out of its back. Then there was a race of giants called **Centimanes**, each of which had 50 heads, and a dragon called Ladon that had 100 heads!

⬆ *Cerberus, the three-headed dog.*

Myth-makers in other parts of the world have also told tales about many-headed creatures. The **Vikings** of Scandinavia created myths about a six-headed giant called Thrudgelmir. He was said to be one of the first beings ever to have lived on Earth.

⬅ *The Hydra, from ancient Greek myth, was a deadly, multi-headed serpent.*

➡ *Thrudgelmir was a six-headed monster of the Vikings.*

Terrifying Typhon

Of all the monsters of ancient Greece, Typhon was the most terrifying. He had the body of a snake, huge dragon wings and fiery eyes. The god Zeus locked him away beneath the volcano Mount Etna, Sicily.

➡ *This ancient Greek vase shows the god Zeus attacking Typhon, a huge, snake-like monster.*

In the folktales of Scotland is a terrifying **ogre** called Red Etin. Not only did he have three heads, but he was also a **cannibal** that caught and ate people.

All these monsters were thought to be so dangerous that they could kill. Only the bravest of the brave would dare to fight them.

⬆ *A Centimane was a scary, multi-headed giant from ancient Greece.*

⬅ *The three-headed ogre Red Etin of Scottish folktales.*

Once upon a time:
How Heracles killed the Hydra

• GREECE

This myth comes from…

⬇ *The Hydra's heads grew back as fast as Heracles cut them off.*

Long ago, people from ancient Greece talked of the greatest hero who had ever lived. His name was Heracles. He had been set 12 difficult tasks. One of them was to destroy the hideous Hydra.

The Hydra was a giant serpent with many heads – some said five, some said 100. Its blood was poisonous, and so was its stinking breath. When the Hydra slithered from its swampy home, nothing was safe.

Heracles went to the Hydra's **lair**, as it was his duty to kill it. When the Hydra appeared, Heracles attacked its heads. But, as soon as he cut off one head, two new ones grew in its place.

To make his task more difficult, a giant crab kept pinching his feet. Heracles called for help, and Iolaus (*say: ee-oh-lus*), his nephew, joined in the battle. The crab was first to die – Heracles smashed its shell with his foot.

← *Iolaus sealed the Hydra's necks with fire, so its heads could not grow back.*

▼ *Heracles, hero of the ancient Greeks, defeated the monstrous Hydra.*

The Twelve Labours of Heracles

In a moment of madness, Heracles killed his own family. As punishment, he was told to work for King Eurystheus (say: yoo-rees-thee-oos). The king set him 12 labours or tasks, one of which was to kill the Hydra.

Then, Heracles sliced off the serpent's heads, and Iolaus touched the bleeding necks with a burning torch. The heat sealed the wounds so new heads could not grow. One by one the heads fell. When the last was cut off, the Hydra was dead. Heracles sliced open its body and took its poisoned blood to use on his arrow-tips.

Once upon a time:
How Heracles caught Cerberus

Cerberus was a fierce, three-headed dog that guarded the entrance to **Hades**, or the underworld. Heracles, hero of the Greeks, was ordered to capture it.

This was the last of the 12 labours, or tasks, that King Eurystheus had set him to do. The gates to Hades led to a cold, dark place below the Earth, where the souls of the dead were taken. Snake heads sprouted from Cerberus' back, and its tail was a serpent.

Cerberus welcomed souls to Hades, greeting them playfully. However, if any soul tried to leave, the dog ate it up.

➡ *Heracles was bitten by the snake that grew from the back of Cerberus.*

King Eurystheus told Heracles to capture Cerberus alive and bring him to the surface of the Earth. Heracles was forbidden to use weapons, so he had to rely on his own strength.

Heracles entered Hades, but there was no welcome from Cerberus. It pounced, and its tail-snake bit him. Heracles grabbed the monster and squeezed its throats until it nearly suffocated. Heracles bound it in chains and carried it into the world of the living.

⬆ *King Eurystheus took one look at Cerberus and fled in terror.*

⬅ *Aconite looks pretty when it is in flower, but it is poisonous.*

Poison plant

Spit from Cerberus' mouths that fell onto the ground was said to grow into aconite, a poisonous plant. It is known by many names, including monkshood and wolfsbane. It grows in northern parts of the world.

The sight of Cerberus was too much for King Eurystheus, who ran away in fear. Heracles unchained the monster, and it ran back to Hades. As for Heracles, his labours were over.

Serpents and sea monsters

If ever there was a creature that, to a storyteller, would make the perfect monster, it was the snake. In the real world, many snakes are natural-born killers. They can squeeze or poison their victims to death.

↑ *Sailors were terrified of monsters they believed could rise up from the sea and sink their ships.*

What's more, snakes can grow to huge sizes, are found on land and in water, and move without making a sound. In myths, snakes became monstrous serpents. Some were big enough to wrap themselves around the whole world! They had poisonous bites, and some were given lots of heads. A common job for many serpents was to guard treasure or captured people — something they had in common with dragons.

Sinbad's monster

Sinbad the Sailor had many adventures in folktales of the Middle East. In one story, he thought he had come to an island in the middle of the ocean. He went ashore with his men, but when they lit a fire, the 'island' came to life and swam to the bottom of the sea. It wasn't an island, but the Zaratan — a giant sea turtle.

⬆ *The Zaratan was so big that sailors mistook it for an island.*

The sea was often the home of monsters — usually very big ones. Myths of the Middle East described a sea monster so big that sailors thought it was an island. They called it the Zaratan. To European sailors of the Middle Ages (around 800 years ago), there was a sea monster to fear above all others. It was called the **Kraken**, a monster that sank ships and drowned all on board.

⬆ *Giant **squid** were sea monsters that could attack and destroy whole ships.*

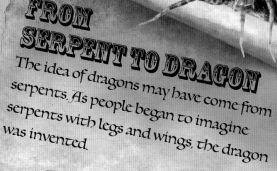

FROM SERPENT TO DRAGON

The idea of dragons may have come from serpents. As people began to imagine serpents with legs and wings, the dragon was invented.

Once upon a time:
The Great Serpent and the flood

• NORTH AMERICA

This myth comes from…

⬆ *The Great Serpent dragged Nanabozho's cousin from their house.*

The Great Serpent is a magical creature from the myths of the Chippewa people of North America.

There was once a hero called Nanabozho (say: *nah-nah-boh-zhoh*), who lived with his cousin. One day, the Great Serpent entered their house, wrapped its coils around Nanabozho's cousin and dragged him away.

Angrily, Nanabozho followed the serpent's tracks to a lake. Far below the water, he saw the monster in its lair, with the dead body of his cousin. Nanabozho called on the Sun to make the water so hot that the Great Serpent would have to come to the surface. Nanabozho hid behind a tree and waited.

This ancient drawing, made on a rock face, shows the Great Serpent.

Great Horned Serpent

Giant snakes are a part of many Native American myths. The Great Horned Serpent comes from stories of the Iroquois people. It is a gigantic rattlesnake that lives in a lake. The Iroquois believe that it protects them when they sail across the water.

Sure enough, the Great Serpent came out of the lake. Nanabozho fired an arrow into its heart, and the serpent fell back into the lake. As it thrashed about, giant waves crashed onto the shore. The land began to flood and covered the whole Earth.

After many days, the water grew calm. It was the sign Nanabozho had been waiting for. The Great Serpent was dead.

➡ *Nanabozho aimed his arrow at the Great Serpent's heart.*

Once upon a time:
Arrow-Odd and the Sea-Reek

This myth comes from…

GREENLAND
ICELAND • • SCANDINAVIA

Sailors in northern seas around Scandinavia, Iceland and Greenland have told tales of a terrifying sea creature called the Kraken.

Long stories, known as **sagas**, were told by the Scandinavians during the Middle Ages. The saga of Arrow-Odd describes a sea monster that sounds very much like the Kraken, called the Sea-Reek.

Arrow-Odd and Vignir were the captains of two ships. One day, they saw two shapes that they thought were rocks rising from the sea. They sailed on, and came to an island they had never seen before. Some of the men went ashore for water. Suddenly, the island sank and the men were drowned.

◄ *The monster slipped beneath the waves, and many men were drowned.*

ANCIENT AMBER

Washed up on some northern shores are pieces of amber – a soft, smooth material that floats. Ancient sailors thought it was Kraken droppings! Today, we know that amber comes from ancient trees.

⬆ *Amber is **resin** from ancient trees, millions of years old.*

Arrow-Odd was deeply troubled. He asked Vignir, who was wiser than him, to explain what had happened. Vignir said they had found the monster Sea-Reek, the biggest monster in the ocean. It swallowed ships and whales, and could stay underwater for days. When it came to the surface, its body floated like an island. Its nostrils stood high above the water – these were the two rocks they thought they had seen. After hearing this, Arrow-Odd continued nervously on his journey.

Kraken close~up

The Kraken was said to measure up to 1.6 km wide. When it swam to the seabed, it made a vast whirlpool. If ships were caught in the swirling waters, they were sucked down to join the monster.

➡ *The swirling water made by the Kraken was enough to drag a ship down to the seabed.*

Monsters with wings

In myths, the land, air and water all have their own monsters. Walking, crawling and slithering monsters live on the land, and the sea is home to swimming monsters. Flying above all these are the monsters of the sky.

Fire-breathing dragons, giant birds and other creatures with wings – the sky is their domain. As long as they stay there, beyond the reach of humans, they are safe. However, when a winged monster comes too close to a human hero, the creature finds itself in trouble.

People have long believed in giant creatures with scaly skin and wings. The ancient Greeks told stories about Harpies – flying creatures with the bodies and wings of vultures and the heads and arms of old women.

⬆ *The **Roc** is said to look like a giant eagle.*

Elephant-carrying bird

The Roc, from Middle Eastern legend, was described as a bird of prey that looked like a giant eagle. It was so big it could carry an elephant in its claws!

18

Harpy

Hippogriff

Roc

Dragon

Griffin

⬆ *Winged monsters were imagined in many different forms, from dragons to giant birds.*

Not all flying monsters are so unreal. The Roc, from Middle Eastern myth, was simply a bird. However, it was much bigger than normal, and that is why it is known as a monster. And, just like other monsters, the Roc was scary because of what it did – it searched for prey to carry off and eat or feed to its young.

Vampires

Blood-sucking **vampires** are flying creatures that exist in the myths of many peoples. For example, the Choctaw tribe of North America describes a creature called the Skatene, and the Tamils of India have the Pey.

⬆ *Vampires feed on the blood of humans.*

Once upon a time:
How Jason defeated the Harpies

This myth comes from…

• GREECE

In the land of the ancient Greeks, Jason was set a difficult task. Pelias, a cruel king, had ordered him to fetch the Golden Fleece – a ram's skin made of gold.

As Jason went in search of the Golden Fleece, he arrived at the city of Salmydessus. A blind man called Phineus lived there, but he was in trouble. Two Harpies – flying creatures that were a cross between vultures and ugly old women – kept swooping down and snatching the food from Phineus' table. This left him forever hungry.

Jason asked Phineus how to find the Golden Fleece. Phineus promised to help on condition that Jason rid him of the Harpies. So Jason and his men, including Zetes and Calais who were able to fly, waited for the beasts to arrive.

➡ *The Harpies swooped to steal food from Phineus, but Zetes and Calais chased them away.*

When the Harpies came, the two men flew at them with swords, and they fled to a faraway island. Freed from the monsters, Phineus could eat in peace. In return, he helped Jason on his voyage to find the Golden Fleece.

⬆ *A Harpy painted on the side of an ancient Greek vase.*

Body-snatchers

The word 'harpy' means 'snatcher'. According to the ancient Greeks, a person lost at sea had been snatched by Harpies. Their human arms ended in the sharp talons of eagles, and once these had closed around a victim, there was no escape. They were surrounded by a terrible smell, and spoiled whatever they touched.

Once upon a time:
The griffins and their gold

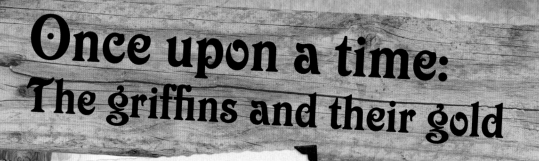

• GREECE

This myth comes from…

Imagine a creature that is part-lion, part-eagle. This mighty beast is called a griffin – an animal with the body of a lion and the head and wings of a bird of prey.

The griffin was a greedy creature with fire-red eyes and large ears. It attacked anything that came near, as it was afraid they might be after the gold that it so jealously guarded.

The griffins fiercely guarded their gold from the thieving Arimaspians.

According to the ancient Greeks, griffins lived in Scythia, a region far to the north of Greece. They lived high up in the snowy mountains, and did so for good reason. The mountains were a source of gold, which the griffins dug up with their claws and beaks. The griffins loved the bright and shiny metal so much that they made their nests from it.

A hippogriff was part-horse and part-griffin. It was friendlier towards humans than griffins were.

ALEXANDER AND THE GRIFFINS

Alexander the Great (lived 356 to 323 BC) was an important general of ancient Greece. It's said he chained eight griffins to a basket. He wanted them to fly him up to the heavens to meet the gods.

A race of one-eyed men called Arimaspians lived at the foot of the mountains. They climbed the mountain tops until they came upon the golden nests. As soon as they stole the gold, the griffins dug more gold and built new nests. The one-eyed thieves came for them again and again.

Hippogriffs

A hippogriff is a beast with the rear of a horse and the front of a griffin. Unlike the wild griffins, hippogriffs can be tamed and used to carry human riders through the sky.

Humanoid monsters

Perhaps the scariest of all mythical monsters are the ones that look like humans. However, look closer and it's obvious they're not human at all. They are **humanoids** – creatures that have a mixture of human and non-human parts.

Humanoid monsters have existed in myths for thousands of years. For example, more than 3000 years ago, the people of ancient Iraq believed in a hideous giant called Humbaba. His face was a mass of coiled intestines, or guts.

Clay models of his face were hung inside houses. This was supposed to keep evil away. Perhaps evil was scared of Humbaba because he was so ugly!

⬆ *Humbaba looked like a giant, hideous human.*

➡ *In Jewish legend, the golem was a human-like creature made of clay.*

Humanoids also existed in the myths of the ancient Greeks. The **gorgons** were three terrifying sisters. One sister, called Medusa, had fangs in her mouth and her head was covered in snakes. If you looked into her eyes, you were turned instantly to stone.

↑ *Medusa was a female monster whose gaze could turn people to stone.*

Frankenstein's Monster

Humanoid monsters also appear in books. One of the best-known monsters was invented in 1818 by Mary Shelley. She described how a scientist, called Victor Frankenstein, made a monster from human body parts. His terrifying creation is known as 'Frankenstein's Monster'.

← *The Minotaur, from ancient Greek myth, had the body of a man and the head of a bull.*

Myths tell of humanoid monsters that existed alongside humans. The stories mixed real-life places with made-up monsters. This caught people's attention, and they went away believing that these monsters really did exist.

Once upon a time: Theseus and the Minotaur

This myth comes from...

• GREECE

Long ago, on the Greek island of Crete, lived a flesh-eating monster called the Minotaur. It was part-man, part-bull.

The Minotaur was the prisoner of Minos, the king of Crete. He kept the beast in a great building called the **Labyrinth** (say: *la-ba-rinth*). Inside was a maze of passages from which there was no escape.

Every year, a ship sailed from Athens to Crete. On board were seven young men and seven young women, who were gifts from the people of Athens. Minos sent them into the Labyrinth, and one by one the Minotaur ate them.

Bull-leapers

The early people of Crete are known as Minoans, after Minos. Bulls were important to them. A wall painting at the palace of Knossos shows how they used to somersault over bulls by grabbing their horns.

➡ *This wall painting shows Minoans leaping over a bull.*

The real labyrinth

The palace at Knossos, Crete, was built about 1500 BC. When archaeologists uncovered it hundreds of years later, they discovered it had about 1000 rooms joined together. Its maze of rooms might have given Greek storytellers the idea for the Labyrinth.

⬆ *The ruins of the palace at Knossos, Crete, showing its maze of rooms.*

One year, Theseus asked to be picked. He wanted to kill the Minotaur once and for all.

On Crete, Theseus met Ariadne, the daughter of King Minos, who gave him a ball of wool. Theseus unwound the wool as he walked inside the Labyrinth. There, he met the Minotaur, and struck it dead. Theseus followed the wool back to the entrance, took Ariadne and the Athenians with him, and set sail for home.

⬇ *Inside the Labyrinth, Theseus came face-to-face with the Minotaur.*

Once upon a time:
The old woman and the Flying Head

This myth comes from…

• USA

A very odd humanoid monster exists in the folk tales of the Iroquois Native American people. It is known as the Flying Head.

That's all it is – a huge, wrinkled head with black wings for ears, fiery eyes, wild hair and sharp teeth.

The Flying Head flies at night. It moans as it rushes towards sleeping humans, especially women and children. It beats its wings against their homes and then, after a few days, someone in the house dies. This is because the Flying Head is the messenger of death.

The Flying Head was hungry for the old woman's acorns.

The Iroquois lived in fear of the Flying Head. One night, it visited the lodge of an old woman. She had lived a long life, and wisdom was her strength. She knew the monster would come for her, and she prepared herself for it. A fire was always burning in her cabin, and on it the old woman kept a pile of red-hot stones. As she sat by her fire, she roasted acorns for her evening meal.

Native American children listen to a storyteller's tale. In time, they will pass it on to their children.

TELLING TALES

Like all myths, the tale of the old woman and the Flying Head began as a spoken story. The people who heard it told it to their children, who did the same to their children. At some point, the story was written down and printed in a book, and so it was saved for future families to read.

The Flying Head watched the old woman, and when it saw her eat the acorns, it wanted some, too. It flew into the room, but instead of gobbling up the acorns, its mouth closed around the red-hot stones. Nothing could ever fall out of its mouth, and as the fire stones began to burn it, the creature spun around in agony until it died.

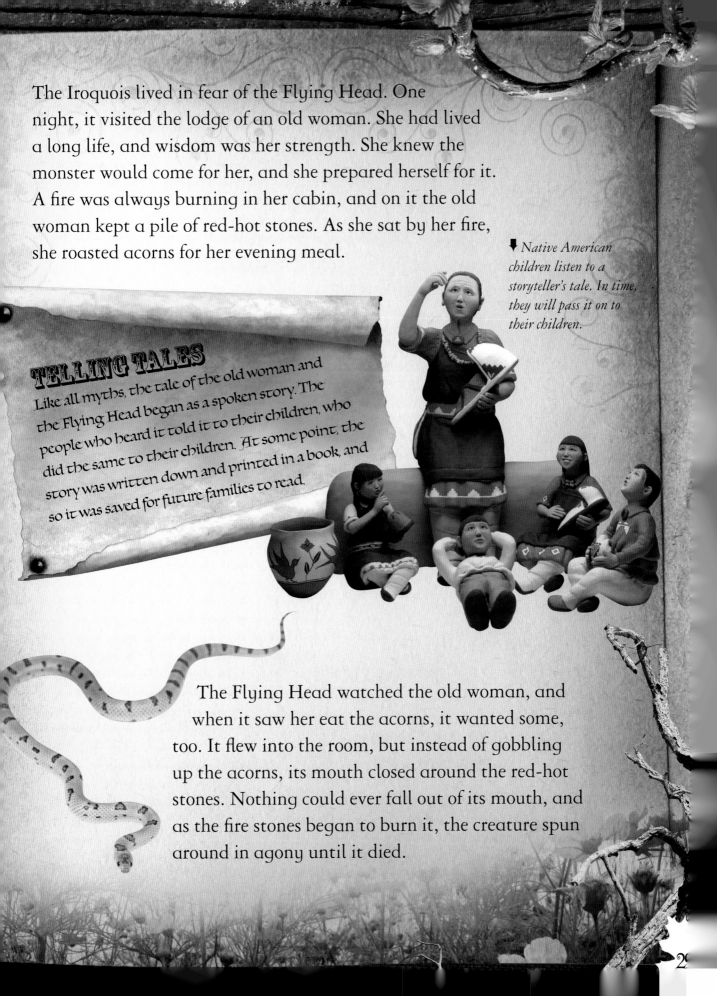

GLOSSARY

Cannibal
A person who eats human flesh, or an animal that eats animals of its own kind.

Centimanes
Giants from the myths of ancient Greece with 50 heads and 100 arms. Also known as Hundred-Handers.

Chimera
A monster from the myths of ancient Greece that was a cross between a goat, a lion and a serpent.

Golem
A humanoid monster from Jewish myths that was formed from clay. It was a servant that helped and protected its human masters.

Gorgon
A humanoid monster from the myths of ancient Greece whose head was covered in snakes. If a person looked into its eyes, they were turned to stone.

Hades
In the myths of ancient Greece, Hades is the Land of the Dead – the place below the earth where the souls of the dead are taken.

Hippogriff
A beast with the rear of a horse and the front of a griffin, from the myths of ancient Greece.

Humanoid
A monster that is similar to a human.

Kraken
A gigantic sea monster from the myths of Northern Europe.

Labyrinth
A confusing maze of rooms and passages in the myths of ancient Greece. At the centre of the Labyrinth lived the Minotaur.

Lair
The place where an animal, often a dangerous one, lives.

Ogre
A male giant from the myths of Europe. A female is an ogress or a hag. Ogres and ogresses are stupid creatures that are easily fooled by humans. They are very strong, and some are said to be cannibals.

Resin
A see-through substance that comes from the sap of trees.

Roc
A giant bird of prey in the myths of the Middle East.

Saga
A long story told by the Vikings about their gods, monsters, kings and history.

Serpent
A very large snake.

Squid
A sea animal, like an octopus, with eight arms and two tentacles.

Underworld
An underground place where the spirits of the dead live.

Vampire
A blood-sucking monster, usually pictured as a bat with fangs.

Vikings
People from Scandinavia (Norway, Sweden and Denmark) whose culture existed from about AD 800 to 1100.

Werewolf
A monster from myths around the world that is said to be able to change from a wolf into a human being, and back again.

INDEX